Presented
to

_____

From

_____

date _____

PICTURE BOOK
of PRAYERS

BEAUTIFUL AND POPULAR PRAYERS
FOR EVERY DAY AND MAJOR FEASTS,
VARIOUS OCCASIONS AND SPECIAL DAYS

By
Rev. LAWRENCE G. LOVASIK, S.V.D.
Divine Word Missionary

CATHOLIC BOOK PUBLISHING CO.
NEW YORK

CONTENTS

Nihil Obstat: Francis J. McAree, S.T.D., Censor Librorum
Imprimatur: ✠ Patrick J. Sheridan, D.D., Vicar General, Archdiocese of New York
The Nihil Obstat and Imprimatur are official declarations that a book or pamphlet is free of doctrinal or moral error. No implication is contained therein that those who have granted the Nihil Obstat and Imprimatur agree with the contents, opinions or statements expressed.

(T-140)

Jesus Teaches Me To Pray

Our Father

OUR Father,
Who art in heaven,
hallowed be Thy Name.
Thy kingdom come,
Thy will be done on earth as it is in heaven.

Give us this day our daily bread,
and forgive us our trespasses
as we forgive those who trespass against us.

And lead us not into temptation,
but deliver us from evil.

Hail Mary

HAIL Mary, full of grace!
The Lord is with you.
Blessed are you among women,
    and blessed is the fruit
    of your womb, Jesus.

Holy Mary,
    Mother of God,
    pray for us sinners,
    now and at the hour
    of our death.

Amen.

Sign of the Cross

IN the name of the Father
and of the Son
and of the Holy Spirit.
Amen.

Glory Be

GLORY be to the Father,
and to the Son,
and to the Holy Spirit.

As it was in the beginning
is now
and ever shall be.

Amen.

Apostles' Creed

I BELIEVE in God, the Father almighty,
creator of heaven and earth.

I believe in Jesus Christ, His only Son, our Lord.
He was conceived by the power of the Holy Spirit
and born of the Virgin Mary.
He suffered under Pontius Pilate,
was crucified, died, and was buried.
He descended to the dead.
On the third day He rose again.
He ascended into heaven,
and is seated at the right hand of the Father.
He will come again to judge the living and the dead.

I believe in the Holy Spirit,
the holy Catholic Church,
the Communion of Saints,
the forgiveness of sins,
the resurrection of the body,
and the life everlasting. Amen.

Angel of God

ANGEL of God,
my Guardian dear,
    God's love for me
    has sent you here.

Ever this day
    be at my side,
    to light and guard,
    to rule and guide.

My dear Guardian Angel,
    keep me from all danger
    and lead me to heaven.

Prayer on Awaking

O MY God,
I offer You
through the Immaculate Heart of Mary
all my thoughts, words, actions, and sufferings
of this day.

I offer them
to please You, to honor You,
and to make up for my sins.

Sweet Mother Mary,
keep me in your care.

Prayers before and after Meals

Before Meals

BLESS us, O Lord,
and these, Your gifts,
which we are about to receive from Your goodness,
through Christ our Lord.

Amen.

After Meals

WE give You thanks,
Almighty God,
for all Your gifts
which we have received through Christ our Lord.

Amen.

Prayers during the Day

DEAR Jesus,
help me to say little prayers to You
during the day:

- Thanks be to God.

- My God and my all.

- Lord, I love You.

- Praised be Jesus Christ.

- Heart of Jesus, I put my trust in You.

- My Jesus, mercy.

- Lord Jesus, bless all the children of the world.

- Holy Mary, pray for us.

Prayer before Going to Bed

MY God and Father,
I thank You for all the blessings
You have given me today.

I am sorry for all my sins,
because they have hurt You.

Bless my father and mother,
my brothers and sisters,
my relatives and friends,
and all who need Your help.

Prayer for Christmas Day

JESUS, my God,
for love of me,
  You were born of the Virgin Mary
  and became a child like me.

You wanted to work and suffer,
  and even to die on the Cross,
  to show Your love for me
  and to save my soul.

When I look into the crib,
  I ask You, Mary, and Joseph
  to bless my family.

When I see the beautiful Christmas tree
  with lights and ornaments,
  I think of how beautiful my soul should be
  in the grace of God
  and that I will live forever.

When I see the toys I received,
  I think of the many wonderful things
  You have done for me.

Thank You, dear Lord,
  for coming on earth
  and dying on the Cross to save the world.

13

Prayer before Going to Confession

JESUS, my Lord and my God,
I am sorry for all my sins
because they have offended You.

You died on the Cross
because of my sins.

I want to try hard
to keep away from sin,
so that I may always be Your friend
and show You that I really love You.

Prayer before Mass and Communion

JESUS, my Lord,
You give Yourself to me
as Food in Holy Communion.

You offer Yourself for me
in every Holy Mass
as You did upon the Cross.

I adore You as my God
in the Sacrament of the Altar
where Your Heart is all on fire
with deepest love for me.

Help me to receive You with love
and to serve You
as You want me to serve You.

Prayer before the Blessed Sacrament

JESUS, I thank You
for staying in the tabernacle
to be with me and to hear my prayers.

You are my best Friend;
I want to visit You often
and tell You that I love You.

O Sacrament most holy,
O Sacrament divine!

All praise and all thanksgiving
be every moment Thine!

Prayer before Studying

DEAR Jesus,
   I want to study hard for You,
      because this is what You want.

Send me Your Holy Spirit
      to give me light and help
      in all my studies,
      especially in my Catechism.

Teach me to know You better,
      to love You more,
      and to help other people love You.

I want You to be
      my best Friend.

Take me to heaven some day.

Prayer for Good Friday

JESUS, I believe that You are my Lord
and my Savior,
   the Redeemer of the human race,
   Who dicd on the Cross
   for the salvation of all people,
   and Who died also for me.

I thank You
   for having suffered and died
   on the Cross
   to make up for my sins
   and to win grace for my soul.

I thank You for having opened heaven
      to me
   by Your death on the Cross.

Jesus, You are my Friend.

You showed how much You love me
   by dying on the Cross for me.

Without You I cannot save my soul.

As You gave Your life for me,
   may I always live my life for You.

Prayer before Going Out To Play

DEAR Jesus,
You were once a child like me
and had friends to play with You.

Bless me and all the friends You gave me.
Help us to be kind to each other
when we play.

Keep us from all that is bad
that we may all be Your friends
and be pleasing to our Heavenly Father.

Prayer when Playing with My Pets

JESUS, I thank You for the many things
You give me that make my life happy.

You give me the little animals
    to be my companions.

They remind me
    of how much You care for me.

I want to be kind to my pets
    and to all animals
    because You made them to give You glory.

Prayer in Time of Joy

MY Lord Jesus,
I am especially happy today
and I thank You that I feel so good.

I also thank You
for all the great things
You have done for me.

Keep me close to You
until I am with You in heaven
where my joy will never end.

Prayer in Time of Holiday

DEAR Jesus,
thank You for letting me live
in this great land.

Help all the citizens of our country
to follow Your holy Will
and to live in love for each other
and for You.

Refresh my mind and body on this day
so that I may continue to serve You
every day of my life.

Prayer for Easter Sunday

JESUS, You are the Son of God,
and You rose from the dead on Easter Sunday.

You saved us from sin and the devil,
   brought us joy and peace,
   and gave us new life and hope.

All the things God the Father made on earth
   are beautiful:
   the sun and sky, fields and meadows,
   flowers and trees, birds and animals.

He made them all for His glory
   and to make us happy.
   But He did not make us for this world;
   He made us for heaven.

I am a child of God.
   You gave me Your own life of grace
   in Baptism.
   My soul is more beautiful in Your eyes
   than the whole world.

Help me to praise the Father
   by being His loving child
   and by loving You as my Brother.

Thanks for My Teachers

LORD, my teachers work hard
to help me learn
many important things I have to know
in my daily life.

Thank You for my teachers,
and all who teach me about You.

They tell me what I must do
to live as a true Christian
and lead other people to You.

Help me to study hard
to please them and especially You.

Thanks for My Friends

JESUS, I thank You for my friends.
You gave them to me
   to make my life happy.

I am sorry I do not always treat them well
   and do not share things with them.

I will try to love the friends
   You gave me.

Bless them, dear Lord,
   and help them to love You.

Thanks for Those
Who Help Us

HEAVENLY Father, I thank You
for all the people
who help us:
doctors, nurses, policemen,
firemen, and many working people.

Help me to be kind to them
and to pray for them.

Bless those who are kind to me,
help them to do their jobs well,
and reward them in heaven someday.

Thanks for Those Who Help Us Pray

D EAR Lord,
bless our Holy Father,
our bishops and priests,
who take Your place among us.

They teach us Your truth,
take away our sins,
and offer Holy Mass.

Help them in their work
for the Church.

Bless all those who teach us
to know and love You.

Reward them in heaven.

Prayer for Pentecost Sunday

HOLY Spirit, my God,
the Third Person
of the Blessed Trinity,
I love You.

You are the Love of God
the Father and the Son.

They sent You to the Church
to make it holy.

I thank You for the grace
You have given me
to make my soul beautiful
and to help me to be good.

Your grace made me a child of God;
it opened heaven to me.

You are the glory of the living
and the hope of the dying;
lead me by Your grace
that I may always be pleasing to You.

Holy Spirit, live in my soul,
and take me to heaven someday.

Prayer for My Family

DEAR Jesus,
I thank You for the good mother and father
You gave me.

I thank You
for my brothers and sisters,
for my home,
for my food and clothes,
and for all the good things I receive.

Grant my parents grace and health on earth
and a great reward in heaven.

Give our family peace and love,
so that we may have a happy home.

Prayer for My Relatives

DEAR Jesus,
You have also given me relatives—
grandparents, aunts and uncles,
and cousins my own age.

When our families get together,
we always have fun,
playing games and laughing a lot.

They are part of my family,
my "extended" family;
help me to be good to them
and make them happy.

Bless all my relatives;
keep them close to You on earth
and take them to heaven at death.

Prayer for Sunday Blessings

DEAR Lord,
Sunday is a special day,
the day of the Lord:
Father, Son, and Holy Spirit.

It is set aside
for us to thank and praise You,
especially at Holy Mass.

Help me to rest from the usual things I do
and think about God
and the things of God.

Make everyone in my family be happy
and let us be good to other people.

Prayer for Weekday Blessings

DEAR Lord,
this day is a gift from You;
   let me make good use of it.

Help me to do what I have to do
   so that I may grow
   in body, mind, and soul.

Every day, let me know You more,
   love You deeper,
   and serve You better
   so that I may be happy with You
   forever in heaven.

Prayer for the Feast of Mary, Mother of God

GOD was pleased to choose you, Mary,
as the Mother of His Son, the Mother of God;
  pray for us, your children.

We admire your dignity and beauty
  and thank God for making you our Mother.

May all the people on earth honor you,
  with all the Saints and Angels in heaven.

Be our Queen and Mother,
  and pray for us to your loving Son.

I entrust my salvation to your care;
  my hope is in your prayers to Jesus
  Who loved to call you Mother.

You are my Mother, too,
  given to me by Jesus on the Cross;
  be a Mother to me and lead me to Jesus.

Prayer To Honor Mary

GOD our Father,
may we always have the prayers
  of the Virgin Mother Mary.
For You bring us life and salvation
  through Jesus Christ her Son.

Psalm 23: Prayer to The Lord my Shepherd

LORD, You are my shepherd;
I have everything I need.
   You give me new strength;
   You guide me in the right way,
   as You have promised.

Even if that way goes through darkness,
   I will not be afraid, Lord,
   because You are with me!

Surely, Your goodness and love
   will be with me as long as I live.
   Your house will be my home forever.

Psalm 26
Prayer of a Good Child

MAKE my heart innocent, Lord,
because I want to do what is right;
I trust in You with all my soul!

May Your great love guide me;
and Your loving care be with me.

Lord, I love the Church where You live,
the place where Your glory dwells,
especially in Holy Communion.

I ask You, Lord, for one thing;
one thing only do I want:
to live in Your presence all my life,
to wonder at Your goodness,
and to ask you to help me.

Psalm 104
Prayer to God the Creator

LORD, my God, how great You are!
You are clothed with majesty and glory;
   You cover Yourself with light.

You created the heavens
   and all the earth with animals and plants;
   the earth is filled with Your blessings;
   You made the sun, the moon, and the stars.

I thank You for the life You gave me,
   and for all the things You do for me;
   I will love You, my God, as long as I live.

Psalm 150
Prayer of Praise to the Lord!

PRAISE God in His glory!
Praise His power in heaven!
Praise Him for the mighty things He has done!
Praise His wisdom and greatness!

Praise Him with trumpets and harps!
Praise Him with song and dancing!
Praise Him with bells and music!
Praise Him with joy and laughter!

Praise the Lord, all living creatures.

Prayer for the Feast of St. Joseph

GOOD St Joseph,
you are the foster father of Jesus,
and the husband of the Blessed Virgin.

You took care of the Holy Family;
take care of me and our family.

Keep us from sin and danger.

Help us always to love Jesus and Mary,
and to love each other for God's sake.

I ask you,
by the love you have for them,
pray for peace and love in our family,
that we may serve God in faith and love
and be united with Him in heaven.

St. Joseph,
you are the Patron of the whole Church.

Pray for the Holy Father the Pope,
the Bishops and priests,
and all members of the Catholic Church.

St. Joseph
help me to lead an innocent life,
and keep it safe by your prayers.

Thanks for the World

HEAVENLY Father, I thank You
for the life You gave me
and for all the things You do
to make me happy in this world.

I thank You for the stars and sky,
for hills and fields and lakes,
for flowers, trees and grass,
for birds and all the animals.

You made all these things.

Never let me forget Your great love for me.

Thanks for My Country

LORD God,
I give You thanks
for letting me live
in this great land,
which is filled with good things.

Thank You
for letting me be free
to live in peace
and to worship You without fear.

Take care of our President
and let him be a good ruler.

Watch over our other leaders in government
and help them to make just laws.

Thanks for My Home

GOD, my loving Father,
I thank You for my home
where I spend most of my life,
and where my parents and family
show me their love.

Thank You for the things I like at home,
where I spend so many happy hours
with those I love very much.

Thank You for the home that protects me
in heat and cold and rain,
and where I work and sleep and play;
where I talk, laugh, eat, and drink;
where so many wonderful things happen to me,
and where I am safe.

Thanks for My Toys

DEAR Jesus,
I thank You for the toys my parents give me.

When You were a Child,
   I am sure that You also had toys
   that Your Mother Mary and St. Joseph gave You.

When I play with my toys,
   I feel very happy
   and close to You,
   dear Jesus.

I know
   that many children in the world are poor
   and have no toys to play with.
   Please help these children.

Thanks for the Television

LORD, You know how much fun I have
watching television.

I also learn a lot,
    and enjoy good stories and cartoons.

Thank You for all the actors,
    singers, musicians, and dancers,
    and the beautiful scenes of nature in color.

Lord, please keep me from watching
    the things I should not see or hear;
    let television make me a better person
    and not do me any harm.

Thanks for the Bible and Prayer Books

HEAVENLY Lord,
 thank You for giving us the BIBLE,
 which is the Word of God.

It is the written story of Your actions in the world
 and the teachings of Jesus, Your Son;
 let me read my Bible stories often.

Thank You also for the Prayer Books,
 which help us learn to speak to You
 and also tell us about Your Church
 and her teachings.

Help me to make good use of these books
 so that I may get closer to You.

Prayer to Christ the King

TEACH me, teach me, dearest Jesus,
in Your own sweet loving way
all the lessons of Your goodness
I must live by every day.

Teach me kindness, dearest Jesus,
which has always filled Your Heart,
not in words and actions only,
but the kindness of the heart.

Be my Friend, O dearest Jesus;
teach me ever to obey,
love my God and love my neighbor,
always faithful to Your way.

Keep me near You, dearest Jesus,
always in Your holy sight.
Draw me to Your Heart, and lead me
in the pathway of Your light.

Hold my hand and help me onward
through the troubles of each day;
let me see You, hear You, feel You
as I try to walk Your way.

When my life on earth is ended,
fill my heart with holy love,
and with all my sins forgiven,
take me to Your home above.

Prayer on
My First Communion Day

JESUS, I believe that Holy Communion
is Your Body and Blood—
   You Yourself, God and Man—
   though it looks like bread and wine.

The bread and wine was changed
   into Your Body and Blood by You
   through Your priest at Mass.

In Holy Communion You come to me
   to give life to my soul,
   and make me more like You
   so that I may have eternal life in heaven.

Prayer on
My Confirmation Day

SPIRIT, God of holiness,
come with grace my soul to bless.
Help my weakness, shed Your light,
make me holy in Your sight.

Through Your love by which I live,
all my sinfulness forgive.
Guide me on the way of right;
help me walk in Your pure light.

God the Father, God the Son,
God the Spirit, ever one!
Give me now Your saving grace,
that in heaven I see Your face.

Prayer on My Birthday

DEAR Jesus, I thank You
for each day of my life;
it is a gift from You.

Help me to use it well to serve You
and the people I meet each day.

Thank You especially for this day,
which is my birthday, my special day.

It reminds me
of the great love You have for me—
a love that gave me life
and many other good things.

When my life on earth is over,
take me to heaven
to live with You forever.

Prayer on My Name Day

DEAR Saint, N.,
I have been honored to bear your name,
which you made famous by your holiness.
Help me never to shame this name.

Obtain God's grace for me
    that I may grow in faith, hope, and love,
    and all the virtues.

Grant that by imitating you I may imitate
    your Lord and Master, Jesus Christ.

Watch over me all my life
    and bring me safe to my heavenly home.

Prayer for Needy Children

LORD, there are many children
who do not have a home
because they are too poor.

Some are homeless and lonesome
because they have no parents,
or have lost their home
because of war, or floods
or earthquakes.

Lord,
please help all those children
and all people who need a home
and food and clothes.

MAGNIFICENT EDITIONS THAT BELONG IN
EVERY CATHOLIC HOME

FIRST MASS BOOK—Ideal Children's Mass Book with all the official Mass prayers. Colored illustrations of the Mass and the Life of Christ. Confession and Communion Prayers. **Ask for No. 808**

PICTURE BOOK OF SAINTS—By Rev. L. Lovasik, S.V.D. Illustrated Lives of the Saints in full color for Young and Old. It clearly depicts the lives of over 100 popular Saints in word and picture. **Ask for No. 235**

MY FIRST PRAYERBOOK—By Rev. Lawrence G. Lovasik, S.V.D. Beautiful new prayerbook that provides prayers for the main occasions in a child's life. Features simple language, easy-to-read type, and full-color illustrations. **Ask for No. 205**

THE MASS FOR CHILDREN—By Rev. Jude Winkler, OFM Conv. New beautifully illustrated Mass Book that explains the Mass to children and contains the Mass responses they should know. It is sure to help children know and love the Mass. **Ask for No. 215**

LIVES OF THE SAINTS—New Revised Edition. Short life of a Saint and prayer for every day of the year. Over 50 illustrations. Ideal for daily meditation and private study. **Ask for No. 870**

CATHOLIC PICTURE BIBLE—By Rev. L. Lovasik, S.V.D. Thrilling, inspiring and educational for all ages. Over 110 Bible stories retold in simple words, and illustrated in full color. **Ask for No. 435**

St. Joseph FIRST CHILDREN'S BIBLE—By Father Lovasik, S.V.D. Over 50 of the best-loved stories of the Bible retold for children. Each story is written in clear and simple language and illustrated by an attractive and superbly inspiring illustration. A perfect book for introducing very young children to the Bible. **Ask for No. 135**

The STORY OF JESUS—By Father Lovasik, S.V.D. A large-format book with magnificent full colored pictures for young readers to enjoy and learn about the life of Jesus. Each story is told in simple and direct words. **Ask for No. 535**

WHEREVER CATHOLIC BOOKS ARE SOLD